ACRED

SING-ALONG SERIES

GOSPEL

Sing-Along Songbook

Arranged by Anna Laura Page & Jean Anne Shafferman

ve Medleys

r 2-Part

Mixed Voices

ith Unison

ongregational

ongsheets

Contents

The publisher hereby grants permission to reprint only pages 36-40 for the purpose of performance with the congregation provided that a sufficient quantity of copies is purchased for the choir.

www.alfred.com

Cover photo courtesy of PhotoDisc, Inc.

Songbook (19969) ISBN 0-7390-1686-5   Preview Pack (19970) ISBN 0-7390-1687-3
Choir Kit (19971) ISBN 0-7390-1688-1   Accompaniment/Performance CD (19972) ISBN 0-7390-1689-X
Listening CD (19973) ISBN 0-7390-1690-3

Foreword

The Sacred Sing-Along Series

Choirs and congregations alike will love the *Sacred Sing-Along Series*. Each collection in this series includes popular traditional favorites arranged in medleys for 2-part mixed choir with unison congregational singing. Reproducible congregational songsheets, featuring both melody and lyrics, are included in each songbook.

For Traditional and Praise Worship

A wonderful source of "emergency anthems," this series offers inspiring arrangements that are quickly and easily prepared. Great for summer worship and appropriate for use throughout the year, this series is certain to become an indispensable addition to your choral library, and a popular favorite with your choir!

For Congregational Singing

The unique sing-along format with reproducible songsheets is ideal for informal Christian fellowship events. Use them for congregational dinners or retreats, Sunday school programs, church camps, revivals and praise gatherings.

The Gospel Sing-Along Songbook

This first installment in the series, the *Gospel Sing-Along Songbook*, offers a vital link to our rich Christian musical heritage. It includes five medleys incorporating twelve timeless classics by some of the greatest gospel musicians and poets of the nineteenth and early twentieth centuries. Program these medleys for a hymn sing in worship. Teach them to and perform them with children. For a complete listing of titles, composers and lyricists, as well as corresponding scripture readings and applications to the liturgical worship service, please see the *Songbook Summary* below.

The *Gospel Sing-Along Songbook* is available individually, No. 19969, or in a handy, money-saving Choir Kit, featuring ten Songbooks and one Full Performance/Accompaniment CD recording, No. 19971. Additional components include the Preview Pack (1 Songbook and 1 Listening CD), No. 19970, and separate Full Performance/Accompaniment CD (No. 19972) and Listening CD (No. 19973) recordings.

Songbook Summary

1. IN THE SWEET UP YONDER

Sweet By and By—*Words by Sanford F. Bennett (1836-1898)*
Music by Joseph F. Webster (1819-1875)
When the Roll Is Called Up Yonder—*Words & Music by James M. Black (1856-1938)*

Suggested corresponding scripture readings include John 14: 1-6, 1 Corinthians 15: 50-57 and 1 Thessalonians 4: 13-18. This medley is especially appropriate for All Saints', Ascension, Christ the King and funeral services.

2. MEDLEY OF THE CROSS

The Old Rugged Cross—*Words & Music by George Bennard (1873-1958)*
Jesus Paid It All—*Words by Elvina M. Hall (1820-1889)*
Music by John T. Grape (1835-1915)
Near the Cross—*Words by Fanny J. Crosby (1820-1915)*
Music by William H. Doane (1832-1915)

Suggested corresponding scripture readings include Mark 10: 15, Philippians 2: 5-11, Hebrews 5: 5-11, Galatians 6: 11-15 and Revelation 7: 9-17. This medley is especially appropriate for Lent and Holy Week.

3. JESUS, HAVE THINE OWN WAY

I Must Tell Jesus—*Words & Music by Elisha A. Hoffman (1839-1929)*
Have Thine Own Way, Lord—*Words by Adelaide A. Pollard (1862-1934)*
Music by George C. Stebbins (1846-1945)

Suggested corresponding scripture readings include Psalm 55: 22, Isaiah 64: 8, Matthew 6: 25-34, Luke 12: 22-34 and Revelation 4: 14-21. This medley is especially appropriate for evangelism, Lent and stewardship.

4. STORIES OF JESUS

Tell Me the Old, Old Story—*Words by A. Catherine Hankey (1834-1911)*
Words by William H. Doane (1832-1915)
I Love to Tell the Story—*Words by A. Catherine Hankey (1834-1911)*
Music by William G. Fischer (1835-1912)
We've a Story to Tell to the Nations—*Words & Music by H. Ernest Nichol (1862-1928)*

Suggested corresponding scripture readings include Matthew 4: 23-25 and 24: 14, John 3: 16 and 15: 9-17, Acts 8: 4-8 and 1 John 4: 7-19. This medley is especially appropriate for Ascension, Christ the King, evangelism and stewardship.

5. STANDING AND LEANING

Standing on the Promises—*Words & Music by R. Kelso Carter (1849-1928)*
Leaning on the Everlasting Arms—*Words & Music by Elisha A. Hoffman (1839-1929)*

Suggested corresponding scripture readings include Deuteronomy 33: 26-29, Psalm 90: 1-2 and 2 Peter 1: 1-4. This medley is especially appropriate for Ascension, Christ the King, evangelism and stewardship.

1. IN THE SWEET UP YONDER

Sweet By and By / When the Roll Is Called Up Yonder

for 2-part mixed voices, accompanied

Arranged by
ANNA LAURA PAGE *and*
JEAN ANNE SHAFFERMAN

6

22 **When the Roll Is Called Up Yonder**

19969

31 **Sweet By and By**

10

19969

2. MEDLEY OF THE CROSS

The Old Rugged Cross / Jesus Paid It All / Near the Cross

for 2-part mixed voices, accompanied

Arranged by
ANNA LAURA PAGE *and*
JEAN ANNE SHAFFERMAN

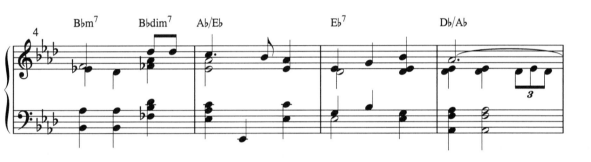

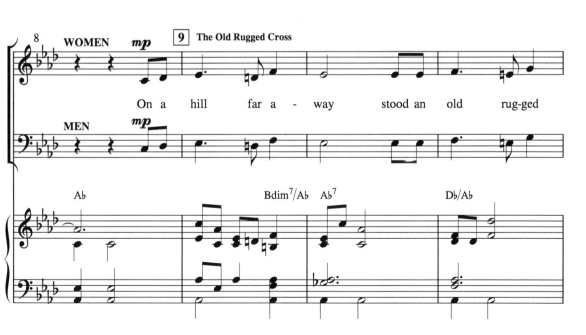

19969

37

poco rit.

change it some - day for a crown.

Ab/Eb   Eb7   Ab   Bb7

cresc.   poco rit.

41 a tempo   (mel.) mf   **43** Jesus Paid It All

I — hear the Sav-ior say: "Thy strength in-deed is

Eb   Cm   Fm7   Bb7

mf a tempo

46

small. Child of weak - ness, watch and pray; Find in Me thine all in

mp   mf

Oh;

Eb   Abmaj7/Bb   Eb   Cm   Abm   Eb   Bb7

3. JESUS, HAVE THINE OWN WAY

I Must Tell Jesus / Have Thine Own Way, Lord

for 2-part mixed voices, accompanied

Arranged by
ANNA LAURA PAGE *and*
JEAN ANNE SHAFFERMAN

17

Je - sus! I must tell Je - sus! Je-sus can help me, Je-sus a-

C   Am⁷   F♯dim⁷   G♯dim⁷ Am   A♭⁷   C/G   Am   Dm⁷ G⁷

20

lone.

mf (mel.)

Have Thine own

C   F/C   C   C/G

22 Have Thine Own Way, Lord
mp (2nd time only)

2. Have Thine own way,   Lord!   Have Thine own way,   Lord!

(1.) way,   Lord,   have Thine own   way!   Thou art the
(2.) way,   Lord,   have Thine own   way!   Wound-ed and

F/C   C   D⁷/C

mf

31 I Must Tell Jesus

4. STORIES OF JESUS

**Tell Me the Old, Old Story / I Love to Tell the Story /
We've a Story to Tell to the Nations**

for 2-part mixed voices, accompanied

Arranged by
ANNA LAURA PAGE *and*
JEAN ANNE SHAFFERMAN

39 We've a Story to Tell to the Nations

We've a sto-ry to tell to the na- tions that shall turn their hearts to the right: a sto - ry of truth and__ mer - cy, a sto - ry of peace and

come on earth, the king-dom of love and light; _____ and

Christ's great king-dom shall come on earth, the

king-dom of love and light! _____

5. STANDING AND LEANING

Standing on the Promises / Leaning on the Everlasting Arms

for 2-part mixed voices, accompanied

Arranged by
ANNA LAURA PAGE *and*
JEAN ANNE SHAFFERMAN

Leaning on the Everlasting Arms

What a fel - low-ship, what a joy di-vine,

lean - ing on the ev - er - last - ing arms. What a bless-ed-ness,

Stand - ing,

what a peace is mine, lean - ing on the ev - er - last - ing arms.

stand - ing,

34

1. IN THE SWEET UP YONDER

Sweet By and By / When the Roll Is Called Up Yonder

for congregation

Arranged by
ANNA LAURA PAGE *and*
JEAN ANNE SHAFFERMAN

2. MEDLEY OF THE CROSS

The Old Rugged Cross / Jesus Paid It All / Near the Cross

for congregation

Arranged by
ANNA LAURA PAGE *and*
JEAN ANNE SHAFFERMAN

3. JESUS, HAVE THINE OWN WAY

I Must Tell Jesus / Have Thine Own Way, Lord

for congregation

Arranged by
ANNA LAURA PAGE *and*
JEAN ANNE SHAFFERMAN

4. STORIES OF JESUS

Tell Me the Old, Old Story / I Love to Tell the Story /
We've a Story to Tell to the Nations

for congregation

Arranged by
ANNA LAURA PAGE and
JEAN ANNE SHAFFERMAN

5. STANDING AND LEANING

Standing on the Promises / Leaning on the Everlasting Arms

for congregation

Arranged by
ANNA LAURA PAGE *and*
JEAN ANNE SHAFFERMAN